STOKED

*7 STRATEGIES FOR KINDLING & KEEPING
YOUR FIRE FOR GOD
WHILE IN CHRISTIAN COLLEGE*

WRITTEN BY
DANIEL DAY

Unless otherwise noted, scripture quotations are used by permission, with all rights reserved, from the following sources:

Scripture quotations noted ESV are from The Holy Bible, English Standard Version® (ESV®), copyright © 2001 by Crossway, a publishing ministry of Good News Publishers. Used by permission. All rights reserved.

Scripture quotations noted NIV are from the Holy Bible, New International Version®, NIV®. Copyright ©1973, 1978, 1984 by Biblica, Inc. ™ Used by permission of Zondervan. All rights reserved worldwide. www.zondervan.com

Scripture quotations noted NKJV are from the New King James Version®. Copyright © 1982 by Thomas Nelson, Inc. Used by permission. All rights reserved.

Scripture quotations noted KJV are from the King James Version.

ISBN 0-7414-5904-3

Printed in the United States of America

The names of some individuals whose stories are told in this book have been changed to protect their privacy.

Published March 2010

INFINITY PUBLISHING
1094 New DeHaven Street, Suite 100
West Conshohocken, PA 19428-2713
Toll-free (877) BUY BOOK
Local Phone (610) 941-9999
Fax (610) 941-9959
Info@buybooksontheweb.com
www.buybooksontheweb.com

ENDORSEMENTS

"Daniel Day, in his book STOKED, has addressed one of the most important issues for any student pursuing Christian education: Endurance. He is young enough to speak the language of the student, but mature enough to discern practical and spiritual solutions. The seven principles in this book can save a student from needless discouragement or disillusionment. I highly recommend it for the prospective student entering a Christian college or university."

— M. Wayne Benson,
President and CEO of Emerge Ministries

"Daniel Day has addressed one of the great potential challenges facing many Christian college students today: maintaining one's passion for God in the face of the ever-present pressure to cruise, conform or compromise. STOKED provides practical insight and a refreshing perspective for those beginning this academic and spiritual journey. Well worth the read!"

— C. Ronald Bradley,
**Senior Pastor
NewSong Church - Cleveland Heights, OH**

-ENDORSEMENTS-

-ENDORSEMENTS-

"Every spiritual spark has the potential to become a flame. Every flame needs fuel to burn. The flame of a relationship with Jesus must be nurtured and not neglected. In STOKED Daniel Day challenges students heading-off to Bible college with practical instruction on how not to neglect the care of their call and most importantly their relationship with Christ. This is an engaging must-read for every Christian entering college regardless of their major."

— Dr. Garland Owensby,
Professor, College of Bible and Church Ministries
Southwestern Assemblies of God University

"I was totally STOKED after reading Daniel Day's new book. It's great counsel for students attending a Christian college or, for that matter, any college or university where they will be surrounded by others who might dampen or destroy their faith. Keeping your faith on fire is what this book is all about!"

— Donald Cartledge,
Director, Cincel Language School,
San Jose, Costa Rica

"Daniel does an excellent job laying out some fundamentals that will help guide you through your Christian college experience so that you finish without regret and without losing your passion for Jesus. You will enjoy the personal stories from a guy who recently sat where you sit and experienced what you are now going through. Daniel has put into book form what he, I, and so many other leaders found to be true in Christian college. Finish strong!"

— Chris Murdoch,
District Youth Director of West Texas

ACKNOWLEDGEMENTS

There are so many wonderful people who have walked along side me over the course of the last year who have helped to make this book a reality. Without their help, I know that you would not be holding this finished work in your hands.

Thanks first and foremost to God who planted the desire in my heart to write this book through a time of fasting and prayer. I give all glory and honor to his name. Amen!

Thanks to my wife Sara. Had you not believed in me the way that you always have, I know I would have given up a long time ago. When you believe in me, I know I can accomplish anything.

Thanks to C. Ron Bradley, Dr. Gary A. Denbow, and M. Wayne Benson. The three of you have invested yourselves into me in many ways over the years, and I am eternally grateful. Your lives embody what it means to be continually passionate for Jesus Christ. May you always be stoked.

Thanks to Tim Allen, Barbara Howard, and Sara Day. Without your help on the editing end of this project, I know that there would have been no possibility that this book would have ever come to be.

Thanks to Nick Poole. Your design and layout work on this project has been phenomenal. Thank you for your patience with me and continually putting your heart and soul into your work. Thank you for your friendship over the years, and I look forward to working with you again in the future.

Thanks to Smartt Assembly, Grace Assembly, and Trinity Assembly. Your investment in this project will reap an eternal reward. Thank you for believing in me and the countless thousands of students who will be touched by this book.

STOKED

7 STRATEGIES FOR KINDLING & KEEPING YOUR FIRE FOR GOD WHILE IN CHRISTIAN COLLEGE

WRITTEN BY
DANIEL DAY

To my wife Sara. Without your encouragement, support, and love this book would have never come to be. I love you.

CONTENTS

-INTRODUCTION-

On a warm spring day in 2003, my father and I climbed into our white '89 Oldsmobile Cutlass Cierra and drove the more than 600 miles from our Tennessee home to Springfield, Missouri. At the age of 20, I was passionate for God and extremely excited about the call to ministry on my life. My father and I were traveling to Missouri because I had been accepted into one of the finest Christian colleges in the nation, and we were going to participate in their spring College Days events. On this 8-hour trip, which seemed to last for 16, my father and I were able to have some great conversation, but I can only remember one thing in particular. As we were passing through the Mark Twain National Forest he said to me, "Daniel, don't let Christian College take away your passion for God." I did not understand exactly what he meant or why he chose that time in particular to say those words. My father, who had been in the ministry for more than 25 years at the time, knew more than I did about the real world experiences I was about to face, and he knew I was in for a rude awakening. (Those of you who have been to a Christian college probably know where this is headed).

We arrived that afternoon to an electric atmosphere. Hundreds of potential young ministers were lined up to check in for the weekend events. Everything was going great. People were smiling, introducing themselves, and being extremely helpful. In the course of just a few minutes, I had made two or three new friends from different parts of the country, and we were all overwhelmed with a sense of expectation as to what was about to unfold. We gathered in a small auditorium to enjoy some worship and orientation. The band was alive, loud, and inspiring. The guest speaker made me feel on top of the world, and I knew in my heart I was in the right place. After I checked in, I received my room assignment in the dorm, and I finally got a glimpse of what my dad meant when he said to not let Christian college steal my passion for God. There, in the dorms that night, my eyes were opened.

Josh, a nice young man who was a freshman at the time, invited me to hang out with him since I didn't know anyone yet. He offered to show me around the campus and introduce me to some of the professors and students. Late that night, long after we should have been asleep, I saw and heard things from some of the guys in the dorm rooms that would have made the hair on your neck stand on end. I was uncomfortable. I could tell that these people made my new friend Josh feel uncomfortable also. Are these men truly studying to be ministers and missionaries? Surely I didn't hear him say that. I know I didn't just see that. I must be hallucinating! But the sad fact was I did see and hear things that confused and even frightened me. That night made a strong impression on me. It made me decide right then and there that my most important responsibility at Christian college was to protect the fire and passion of God in my life.

This yearning inside me to guard my raw, unaltered love for Jesus became the primary mission in my life and the inspiration behind this book. My hope is that together we will be inspired by the biblical and current examples of those whose passion for God did not and has not faded. This book is a catalog of my personal journey, as well as others, whose fire did not falter.

-INTRODUCTION-

As I consider my own journey through Christian college, full time ministry, and life, as well as the journey of those biblical examples discussed in this book, there are seven strategies that will help us achieve our ultimate objective of keeping our passion for God.

1. **Extraordinary Faith:** How would you like to receive a full ride scholarship to college? I am sure you would have been just as excited as I was when I received mine. Find out what God taught me about faith when my scholarship was unexpectedly taken from me.

2. **A Powerful Prayer Life:** You will expect to develop and discover many sets of skills on your way through school. Some of those skills you will have already known and others will be discovered along the way. In this chapter you will see how a seemingly unimportant talent became the catalyst for a strong prayer life.

3. **Godly Friendships:** If you have not discovered this already, you will soon find that not everyone attending your school is living for Christ. In this chapter, see how a poor choice of friendships destroyed my friend's passion for God and turned him from the call on his life.

4. **Personal Investment:** The evidence overwhelmingly points to the fact that those who succeed in college, ministry, and life are those who attain these two parts of the mentorship process: having a mentor and

being a mentor. The active participation in the work of the Lord serves to both kindle and keep our passion for God white hot.

5. Resisting Temptation: This chapter will show you that one of the greatest temptations you will face in college will come disguised as "God's will," but if you succumb to this trap of the enemy, you will find yourself anywhere but in God's will. You will read as I share with you one of the greatest failures of my entire college career and how God used that failure to teach me a very difficult lesson.

6. Never Selling Out: We are nothing without integrity. If we compromise our name, our word, and our character, we have nothing. In chapter 6 you will discover how hard it is to fight the temptation to play the political game of ministry. There is a great peace that comes when you have risen on the promotion of God and not the politics of man.

7. Reflecting All Glory To Jesus Christ: True character is revealed not only in how we handle failure, but also in how we handle success. What do we do when people lift us up and give us the credit for something that only God can do? Those who keep their raw and unaltered love for God know that they must always point back to the ONE who enables their effectiveness in the ministry.

-INTRODUCTION-

I would not presume to teach you anything, but perhaps this book can serve as a sign pointing to those who can teach us all. So I echo the advice that my dad gave me all those years ago. Don't let anything steal your passion for God.

I pray that your love for Him will always burn bright, and that this book will help you discover ways to STOKE your passion for Jesus Christ.

- Daniel Day

PART I

KINDLING YOUR FIRE FOR GOD

CHAPTER 1
THE POWER OF EXTRAORDINARY FAITH

my story

      Several months before Christian college was to become a reality in my life, I was awakened out of a deep sleep early one morning with one thing immediately on my mind: foreign missions. This sudden urgency to do something for the nations of the world was unlike any other feeling I had ever experienced. So I woke up, wiped the sleep from my eyes, and began to pray and ask God what this meant. Was he calling me to personally go into missions? Was he asking me to pray for someone specific who needed help somewhere in the world? I didn't quite understand what was going on at that moment, but then it happened! It was as if the clarity of the Holy Spirit was dropped into my heart, and I knew exactly what he wanted me to do. He wanted me to raise a specific amount of money to help support foreign missionaries around the world. I took some time to thank God for the answer, and then I began to try and figure out how to go about raising the money. There was no way for me to know, at least at that point, how that time of prayer set me on a course that would change my life forever.

-CHAPTER 1-

The year was 2002, and at that time I was the worship leader for a small Assemblies of God church in Tennessee. As a church we gave around $2,000 a month to support various missionaries around the world. (That isn't much compared to some churches, but for us it was a lot!) My goal was to raise half of one month's budget on my own, and I began to call around to other churches and ask if I could come and sing for a love offering to give to missions. My idea worked, and soon many churches began to support my cause. One Sunday night I was singing at a local Baptist church. After the service, a kind, older gentleman came up to me and began to inquire about what my plans were for the future. I told him I was on my way to Christian college after the summer, and I wanted to become a pastor one day. Right then and there, he invited me to have lunch with him later that week. I didn't think a whole lot about it, but then he said something that really heightened my interest. He asked me to bring all of the financial information regarding my future education. He wanted to have a look at it to see if there was anything he could do to help me financially with school. To say that I was excited would have been the understatement of the year. The next thing I knew, we met for one of the most incredible Chinese lunches I have ever eaten.

As we sat down that afternoon to enjoy some sweet and sour chicken with fried rice (oh, that makes me crave some Chinese food), I learned a little bit about this mysterious person who showed up in my life at just the right moment to save the day. I learned that he was an ex-executive of a major foreign car company in Atlanta, Georgia. I also learned that he was extremely wealthy, retired, and very desirous to help young men and women in their pursuit of the call of God on their lives. This was a dream come true! By the end of the meal, not only had he offered to pay for my entire four years of college, but he had also offered to provide a stipend so that I would not have to work while pursuing my degree. I couldn't believe what I was hearing. Was I dreaming? Was I about to wake up and realize that none of it had ever happened? No. This was for real. He met with my parents over dinner that same week, and all of my fears of paying for college were taken away...or so I thought.

Over the course of the next several weeks, we met again and again to confirm the plan and then the unexpected happened. My "knight in shining armor" had a real heart for the Indian reservations in Arizona, and he had planned a trip out West to deliver supplies to a missionary that he supported. Upon his return, he had planned to write me into his will just in case anything happened to him while I went away to Bible school. Then, the day before he was scheduled to return, we received a call that changed everything. That day, returning home, the man that I thought was going to take care of everything unexpectedly died at the wheel of his truck of a massive heart attack.

I was crushed on so many different levels. I was confused about why God would allow this to happen. I was furious and grieved all at the same time. I did not know how to process what I was feeling. This all happened just three months prior to my move to Springfield, Missouri, and I did not have enough money to go to school. My new friend did not have the opportunity to write me into his will. Not only did I lose a friend, but I also lost my free ride through college. Did God call me?

-CHAPTER 1-

Without a doubt, yes. How was I going to pay for school? I had no clue. But as horrible as the situation was, I realized a very important lesson. God is my source, not man. He is my source of hope. He is my source of life. He is my source of faith. And at that moment I decided that if God had truly called me to prepare for the ministry, he would provide all that I needed to succeed.

I am writing this book in the year 2009. I graduated from Christian college, along with my beautiful wife, in May of 2007. As I look back over the course of the last several years, I can truly say that God has been continually faithful to provide everything we have needed. Through God's abundant provision, my wife and I left school with the combined debt of one person who had graduated from a private institution. In the end, God had paid for one of us to go to school for free! But what if I had chosen not to go? What if I had given up on God? My life would be very different now. If we are going to successfully navigate to the end of our journey, we must walk by faith. We must believe that God is more than able to redeem our situations and bring us through the difficult times.

God did it for me. God did it for Jonathan.

-THE POWER OF EXTRAORDINARY FAITH-

Charge The Impossible: JONATHAN'S JOURNEY
-1 Samuel 14:6-

"Jonathan said to his young armor-bearer, "Come, let's go over to the outpost of those uncircumcised fellows. Perhaps the LORD will act in our behalf. Nothing can hinder the LORD from saving, whether by many or by few."

Jonathan has to be one of my all-time favorite people recorded in the Bible for this reason: he had a God-sized perspective. In 1 Samuel 13 and 14, the nation of Israel found itself in a situation that was bleak at best. The fighting men that stood with Saul and Jonathan numbered around 600. They faced an army of Philistines fielding 30,000 chariots, 6,000 horsemen, and foot soldiers that numbered like the sand on the seashore. From a simple, human perspective, anyone would be able to tell who was going to win this battle. No wonder the Israelites were hiding in the caves, holes, rocks, and tombs! But there was one man in the camp that was able to move past the human perspective and look at the problem through the eyes of God. His name was Jonathan. When Jonathan compared the strength of the enemy to the almighty power of God, he knew that he was on the winning side.

Not only were the Israelites outnumbered, but the only swords in the camp belonged to King Saul and Jonathan..The entire Hebrew military was armed with nothing more than glorified farming equipment. And even though Jonathan's army was outnumbered and ill-equipped, he chose to take what he did have and fight. He went on nothing more than faith. He went on nothing more than the hope that the God of his fathers would show up and fight the battle for him. He rose up in courage, along with his armor bearer, and charged the impossible. Just a quick note on this point: even though Jonathan's faith and trust were completely in God, he did not go alone. He took his armor-bearer with him. We should always be willing to take someone with us on our faith journey. This companionship provides the opportunity for our passion for God to be ignited in someone else through whom God might work the impossible. More will be said about the importance of mentoring in chapter 4.

Even with all of his faith, strength, and courage, Jonathan's challenges did not seem to get better before they got much, much worse. He had conquered the first step of faith when he resolved to move ahead, even though the odds were severely stacked against him. He conquered the second step when he picked himself up, took his armor-bearer, and began the hike toward the front line of battle. But Jonathan discovered something on the way that we all eventually discover once we begin a faith journey. He discovered that the road of faith is anything but safe or comfortable, and many times is downright scary. Before Jonathan could even begin his attack, he, along with his armor-bearer, faced one more challenge. He faced a treacherous hike and rock climb down and up two jagged cliffs. And still, in the face of an impossible climb, being grossly outnumbered and armed with one sword and some farming equipment, Jonathan said, "Perhaps the LORD will act in our behalf…" Jonathan charged the impossible…and won the battle!

-THE POWER OF EXTRAORDINARY FAITH-

- Bringing It Home -

If we intend to "make it" in our journey through Christian college, we too must have a God-sized perspective. We too must realize that our God is bigger than our problem, and He is looking for people who will step out in faith and allow him to work in their lives. Even though I faced impossible financial challenges just before I came to Christian college, I knew that God had called me to go, and that was all that mattered. I knew that God was bigger than my financial difficulty. Even though Jonathan was outnumbered, ill-equipped, and faced danger at every turn, he knew that God was bigger than his circumstance. He knew that God was more than able to bring him through the battle successfully.

I know the feeling of being overwhelmed by all of the challenges that can be faced while furthering your education. I know the feeling of being ill-equipped on the journey. I also know the feeling of having to climb through some rough times to reach the other side, but with a God-sized perspective you can navigate any difficulty. You can feel overwhelmed by the academic work, the newfound freedom to come and go as you please, the pressure to be a part of a particular group, and especially the financial cliffs that must be climbed. But I want you to receive this from someone who has been there and knows the faithfulness of our Lord. God will provide for those who charge the impossible. Do not be afraid. Step out in extraordinary faith and watch God work the impossible in your life.

JOURNAL & DISCUSS

1. As it relates to "walking by faith," what has been your greatest single challenge?

_____

_____

_____

_____

2. When have you ever had to "Charge the Impossible" as did Jonathan in 1 Samuel 14:6?

_____

_____

_____

_____

3. Do you have a God-sized perspective when it comes to God providing your every need...financially, emotionally, spiritually, physically, and mentally?

_____

_____

_____

_____

CHAPTER 2
THE POWER OF PASSIONATE PRAYER

my story

When you enter Christian college, you expect to gain many different skill sets that you never had before. On your journey through school, you discover innumerable qualities within yourself that you may not have otherwise found. I can remember very clearly the day I moved into my first dorm room in the fall of 2003. In that moment, I quickly discovered one of these unknown gifts hidden deep within the confines of my mind. Surprisingly, it had nothing to do with my spiritual growth (or so I thought). And what was this hidden talent that I discovered? I found some of the most creative ways to store my stuff! That's right. I learned how to store my clothes, books, boxes, guitars, and all the other random things I owned in the most unusual places. That doesn't sound like a big deal, but when you move into a room that only has one closet to store everything you own, learning how to manage your space becomes a top priority. The most unexpected result of this skill is that it became a major catalyst for some of the greatest moments of prayer in my life.

-CHAPTER 2-

Allow me to give you a mental picture of my new home away from home. The room had brown 1980's carpet, one unmovable desk, one unmovable dresser (that I shared with my roommate), and one closet with one shelf complete with lovely white walls. (Thank God, my alma mater has improved these conditions since then.) Let's just say that the room did nothing for my passion for God. Soon, and I mean really soon, storage space became maxed-out, and not just for me, but also for everyone else on my hall. Each hall had a shared storage closet that filled up almost immediately, so alternative storage facilities were sought out. The place that was chosen as our hall's "catch all" room was a room that may or may not surprise you.

In my dorm, on each hall, there was a room designated for one reason: prayer. The prayer room had the same white walls, the same brown carpet, but this time, instead of a desk and a dresser, it had old wooden altars lining the entire room. These were good-sized rooms, and they were located in the center of the hallway. This location made it extremely convenient and tempting to use the prayer room for storage. Many students began to store their surplus things in these rooms. On any given day, you could walk into these rooms that had been dedicated to prayer and find anything from a mattress to used televisions. They became one-stop markets for just about anything you might want, that is, if you didn't mind the condition in which your items were found. Soon the altars disappeared under the array of random stuff. Then, out of a God-given burden to pray, some of us on the hall took things into our own hands (literally).

-THE POWER OF PASSIONATE PRAYER-

Slowly but surely, my friends and I began the much needed renovation. And with a bit of work, we once again had a quiet place in which to retreat for prayer and meditation. I can remember going into this little sanctuary early in the morning to call on God, and in those moments I learned to hear the voice of God more clearly. The time spent in that place was worth more than any amount of money, prestige, or fame. It was in that place that God forged within me the character I needed to face some of the hardest and most challenging moments of my life. I praise God for the gift of being able to creatively store my property (as well as other people's property), because I know that if I had not spent quality time with God, I could not have survived Christian college with my passion for God intact. If I had not learned to listen to the leading of the Holy Spirit through prayer in those moments, I would have become jaded and skeptical like many other well-intentioned brothers and sisters who walked the same halls as I did.

We must learn to passionately seek the face of God through earnest times of focused prayer if we intend to keep our FIRE through Christian college.

It worked for me. It worked for the prophet Daniel.

Prayer Brings a Spirit of Excellence:
DANIEL'S JOURNEY
-Daniel 6:3-

"Then this Daniel became distinguished above all the other presidents and satraps, because an excellent spirit was in him..."

-CHAPTER 2-

The Bible records in Daniel 6 that King Darius began to delegate the responsibilities of the kingdom to certain presidents and satraps. This was a wise move for him and there is a lesson to be learned here regarding leadership. Any business or leadership book today will tell you that the delegation of powers and responsibilities to the right people is the key to the success of any organization. Darius knew this, and he wanted to set up a leadership team so that the king might suffer no loss (Daniel 6:2).

Jim Collins, in his book Good To Great, says that to be a success you must have the right people serving in the right positions. What a novel idea: the right people serving in the right positions. Disaster could happen for people in leadership if they delegate the wrong person to the wrong position. It would still spell utter ruin for the organization if you get the right people on board but put them in the wrong places. I do not think King Darius read Collins' book, but I do think that Darius would agree with him. This is where Daniel comes into play.

The Bible says that Daniel distinguished himself because of his spirit of excellence. Because of Daniel's faithfulness and attention to detail, he stood out from among the rest. Obviously, Daniel was the best man for the job. He wasn't just a leader, but a leader of leaders. Darius saw this and intended to place Daniel over his entire kingdom, but there were others in the running for the same position, and they plotted to overthrow the king's plans with the hope that they might receive this great honor.

The others plotted and planned to find an accusation against Daniel, but to no avail. They decided that the only way they could trap Daniel would be if they could accuse him in connection to the law of his God (Daniel 6:5). They were right. They advised the king to endorse a law that would trap Daniel into breaking the law of the land and thereby disqualify him for the high position intended for him. The law stated that anyone who prayed to or petitioned any god or man other than Darius for an entire month would be thrown into the den of lions. Daniel, knowing the consequences, continued to pray three times a day. This holy action checked Daniel into the Lion's Mouth Motel for a night, but the Lord protected him. Those who intended to trap Daniel fell into their own trap, and then the Bible records my favorite part of the story. It says in 6:24: At the king's command, the men who had falsely accused Daniel were brought in and thrown into the lions' den, along with their wives and children. And before they reached the floor of the den, the lions overpowered them and crushed all their bones.

- Bringing It Home -

What is a spirit of excellence, and even more importantly, how can we get it? Verse 4 of Daniel chapter 6 gives us some clues. It says, "…They could find no corruption in him, because he was trustworthy and neither corrupt nor negligent". Daniel chapter 1:8 gives us another insight into the heart of this great man of God. It tells us that "…Daniel resolved not to defile himself with the royal food and wine, and he asked the chief official for permission not to defile himself this way". So according to these verses, an excellent spirit from the Lord is exemplified in people who set themselves apart from the world's corruption and character. An excellent spirit can be observed in the faithful work ethic of someone who realizes that they are working not for the world but for the Lord God. But people do not simply wake up one morning and find that they possess a spirit of excellence. There is only one place that someone may find it, and that is in the place of prayer.

Look at Daniel 6:10: *"Now when Daniel learned that the decree had been published, he went home to his upstairs room where the windows opened toward Jerusalem. Three times a day he got down on his knees and prayed, giving thanks to his God, just as he had done before"* (emphasis added). There is no doubt. Daniel was a man of prayer. He was a man of powerful prayer. When you think about it, all Daniel had to do to make sure his promotion took place was to simply take a break from his prayer life. As a matter of fact, all he really had to do was simply pray in the confines of a back room with the door shut. That way, no one would hear his prayers. That would work. Right? Wrong! There was something more important at stake than just saying prayers. This was a war waged on Daniel's most precious time, his prayer time. And he wasn't going to let anyone or anything get in the way of that.

Daniel went to his room, opened the window, and prayed three times a day. My version says it like this. He went to his room, opened the window, and told the enemy to bring it on. Come what may, I am going to pray. Having a prayer life like that will always bring about its inevitable result: an excellent spirit.

Do you intend on finishing Christian college? Do you intend on not only finishing, but also finishing with excellence? An even better question would be, do you intend on being excellent in life and ministry after Christian college? I am sure that you would answer YES to all of these questions. But the fact remains, no one can do it without a prayer life. No one can do it without going to that place of prayer, each day, more than once a day, and seeking the face of Jesus Christ. So I encourage you to take some time right now and evaluate where you are in your prayer life. Do you have a healthy and vibrant time of seeking the face of God each day? If not, follow the example given in Daniel 6 and begin to walk in a spirit of excellence.

JOURNAL & DISCUSS

1. List 5 unsaved people that you are currently praying for and commit to pray for them each day throughout the semester.

_____

_____

_____

_____

2. On a scale from one to ten (ten being the best and one being the worst), how would you rate your "spirit of excellence"?

_____

_____

_____

_____

3. How could you make your prayer times more interactive and creative? Do you keep a prayer journal? Do you have a prayer partner that will keep you accountable? List 3 things that you could do to make your prayer times more enjoyable and less routine.

_____

_____

_____

_____

CHAPTER 3
THE POWER OF GODLY FRIENDSHIPS

1 Corinthians 15:33
"Do not be misled: "Bad company corrupts good character.""

Why did you choose to come to this particular Christian college? Was it because the voice of God spoke to you and said, "You shall come here"? Or was it because they offered a particular major you needed? Maybe you came to this school because they had the nicest campus with facilities complete with beautiful dorm rooms and laundromats conveniently located in each hallway. Attractive tourist spots might be in close proximity to the campus, and that might have influenced your decision. Perhaps you simply came to this institution because it was close to family. Whatever your reason, this I can guarantee: not everyone at this school is here for the right reasons. This was a fact that I had to quickly come to grips with if I had any hope of surviving Christian college.

God confirmed his direction for my life in many different ways and on more than one occasion. I knew that I knew that God had called me to my particular place of preparation, but it only took about a week of living in the dorms to realize that not only were there people at my school who did not appear to be called, there were people in my school who lived as though they didn't know Jesus at all. Granted, these people were the minority, but they were a very vocal minority who knew how to make a lot of noise (at all times of the day and night). One of the most devious strategies that the devil will use to dampen and even destroy the fire in your gut will be to get your eyes *off* of Jesus and *on* this vocal minority.

my story

Take my friend Joe (not his real name) for example. Joe was a good-looking, athletic, and charismatic young man who could make you smile just by walking into the room. He was bright and funny. Many people liked him and fully expected him to complete his studies and go on to do great things for God, but, unfortunately, Joe fell prey to this trap of the enemy: he chose his friends poorly. One day toward the end of my freshman year, I entered the hallway leading to my room to get something for my next class. As I walked through the door I heard someone throwing boxes and other heavy things against the walls and screaming. This did not startle me at first, because honestly, noise was just a part of life in the guys' dorms. There were stacks of trash and wonderful odors that can only be appreciated if you have been there, loud music from multiple rooms, oodles of used Ramen Noodles cups all over the floor, and random people yelling and throwing things. Yes, this was life at its finest in the men's dorms.

The thing that startled me about this particular situation, however, was not that someone was screaming, but what was being screamed. I listened as my friend Joe yelled at the top of his lungs, "I hate this school! I hate this school! Everyone here is a hypocrite!" He said this repeatedly, and I couldn't let it pass. I knew that what he was saying was totally untrue. Not everyone at the school was a hypocrite. I confronted my friend right there in the hallway, calmed him down, and demanded that he explain his words. Something was terribly wrong. If you knew Joe, you would know that he never raised his voice except to praise the Lord. This behavior was totally out of character for him. "What is wrong?" I asked. He repeated his former comments to me, this time softer and with tears. Then I realized that the reason he felt that everyone was a hypocrite was because everyone he hung out with was a hypocrite. He fell into the devil's trap. He took his eyes off of Jesus and put them on the vocal minority who had no business being at a Christian college in the first place. Joe did not finish his degree, and I have no idea where he is now. I cannot help but wonder what his life would have been like if he had just chosen better friends.

Choosing the right friends has everything to do with your success or failure at Christian college and in life in general.

This was true for Joe. This was true for King David.

-CHAPTER 3-

DAVID'S DUMB DECISION
- 1 Samuel 27:1-3 -

"But David thought to himself, "One of these days I will be destroyed by the hand of Saul. The best thing I can do is to escape to the land of the Philistines. Then Saul will give up searching for me anywhere in Israel, and I will slip out of his hand."

So David and the six hundred men with him left and went over to Achish son of Maoch king of Gath. David and his men settled in Gath with Achish. Each man had his family with him, and David had his two wives: Ahinoam of Jezreel and Abigail of Carmel, the widow of Nabal."

Growing weary of the pursuits of his master King Saul, David made a decision that nearly cost him his call as king of Israel. In his distress and anxiety, David chose to run to the land of his enemies so that he might finally "live in peace." The only problem with his plan was that he retreated to the very place that would take away his peace rather than give it. He ran to the land of the enemies of the Lord God, to Gath, in the land of the Philistines. Ironically, he chose the same city which had been home to his first Philistine enemy, Goliath. This would prove to be one of the worst decisions, or should I say dumbest decisions, David ever made.

While David was in the process of moving and reorganizing his militia of 600 fighting men, he immediately made friends with the king of Gath, Achish. Obviously, the king was skeptical, and with reason. This was David, the servant of the king of Israel. The Israelites sang about the great exploits and conquests of David, and those tunes terrorized the Philistine people. Now the one of whom they sang was knocking at the door of King Achish and asking for a home in his kingdom. It seemed strange to the king and even to David's men. The only one who seemed to be unaffected by this uncomfortable situation was David. Therein lays the problem. He was numb to his dumb decision. It took a tragedy to wake him from his stupor.

The battle lines were drawn. Israel and its army were encamped against the Philistine nation. King Achish and his army began the long march to the front lines. Along with Achish, however, was an unexpected crew of soldiers, David and his 600 men. This made the rest of the Philistine commanders very nervous. They wanted Achish to send David back to his home. Achish defended David, but to no avail. The majority ruled that David must leave and return to Ziklag. The disturbing part of this account was not that David was sent back, but that he was angry and offended that he was not able to go to war alongside Achish. He actually wanted to fight against his own people. He wanted to fight the very people that he was to one day rule as king. He was the anointed man of God for the nation of Israel, yet somehow he had gotten to the point in his life where he was willing to go to war against his own nation. How could this happen? What caused this slow deterioration of the heart and mind? We will try to answer that question in a moment, but first, let's find out how the story ends.

Upon returning to the place he once called home, David was not welcomed by his family and friends. Rather, David was greeted by clouds of smoke, smoldering ash, and the silent eeriness of an empty city. His home and the homes of his men had been terrorized and destroyed by the Amalekites. Their families, including their wives and children, had been captured.

1 Samuel 30:6 records the response of David after this horrible affair.

- 1 Samuel 30:6 -

"David was greatly distressed because the men were talking of stoning him; each one was bitter in spirit because of his sons and daughters. But David found strength in the LORD his God."

David found strength in the Lord his God. What a powerful statement! Even in the worst possible moment of David's life thus far, he still knew where to go so that he could find strength and wisdom. In this moment of tragedy, David realized just how foolish he had been to move to the land of his enemies. So David strengthened himself in the only ONE who could bring him hope. He pursued the Amalekites, destroyed them, and rescued his family and everyone else's families as well. But when you think about it, this whole situation could have been avoided if David would have simply surrounded himself with better people.

Let's assess the situation. The anointed future king of Israel retreated from his problems instead of facing them. When he chose to run, he ran to the enemies of God rather than running to God himself. In light of the fact that he made his home with the wrong people, he became influenced by their lifestyles and customs. Because of this terrible situation, David found himself fighting on the wrong side of the battle lines, and if he had had his way, he would have fought and killed his own people. This demoralizing scenario can be traced back to one dumb decision: David made friends with the wrong crowd, and it nearly destroyed his life and the lives of his men.

-THE POWER OF GODLY FRIENDSHIPS-

- Bringing It Home -

We saw clearly in the opening story of this chapter how choosing the wrong friends absolutely devastated Joe's life and calling. It caused him to be jaded, cynical, and bitter. His choice of friends alienated him from those who truly cared about him, and he began to feel isolated, alone, and willing to lash out at his true friends. Rather than running to Jesus and focusing on him, he ran to the enemy, and, unfortunately, they corrupted him into believing and acting the way they did. When I think about the potential that resided within Joe's life, I am grieved because he had so much to offer.

If only he had simply picked better friends.

When you consider your closest circle of friends, you need to ask yourself a few questions.

1. Do they cause you to desire more of God?
2. Do they challenge you to pray more?
3. Do you find yourself uplifted and encouraged by them?
4. After you leave their presence, do you feel guilty because of the time you've wasted?
5. When you are around them, do you find yourself gossiping, backbiting, or slandering other people?
6. Do they make you feel jaded, cynical, and critical towards others?
7. Do your closest friends kindle or kill your fire for God?

This is by no means an exhaustive list of questions that you may ask when determining your circle of influence, but it does give you a start. If you expect to continue through Christian college and make it all the way to the end, you must choose your friends wisely.

We saw two different people in this chapter, Joe and David. Both made the choice to surround themselves with the wrong people. Both faced the potential devastation of that decision. Only one made the right choice in the end. Only one found strength in the Lord his God, and as a result David met his destiny head on. Joe, however, deciding not to find strength in the Lord, destroyed his chances of finishing well in school. Which one will you be?

One Final Thought: Solitary Confinement

While we are still in this vein of thinking, there is one final lesson that I would like to leave with you regarding friendship. Our teacher for this lesson is not David, but the ONE who was called the Son of David. Mark 1:35 says, *"Very early in the morning, while it was still dark, Jesus got up, left the house and went off to a solitary place, where he prayed."* (emphasis added). In this passage, Jesus teaches us one of the most powerful lessons about friendship. Sometimes we just have to get away from everyone. It is not healthy to always be around a group. In Christian college, and throughout your life in ministry, there will be groups of people pressuring you for your undivided attention. If you expect to keep your fire for God through school and ministry, you must learn to cultivate the ONE relationship that matters most, your relationship with Jesus.

-THE POWER OF GODLY FRIENDSHIPS-

So take time to "disconnect." Turn off the cell phone, log out of Facebook, turn off the computer, get alone in your prayer closet, and passionately seek the face of God. Disconnect from the world and connect with Heaven. If we take time to keep this friendship strong, the Bible tells us that God will make even our worst relationships work well. Proverbs 16:7 states, *"When a man's ways are pleasing to the LORD, he makes even his enemies live at peace with him."*

JOURNAL & DISCUSS

1. List your top five friends on campus.

_____

_____

_____

2. Review the questions beginning on page 24. How do your top five friends measure up to those questions?

_____

_____

_____

3. Ask yourself honestly: "Are you currently in a relationship right now that you need to end?"

_____

_____

_____

4. Do you regularly schedule times to get away from everything and everyone so that you can spend uninterrupted time with God?

_____

_____

_____

CHAPTER 4
THE POWER OF PERSONAL INVESTMENT

As we begin this next chapter together, I want you to sit back for a moment and think. Take the next few moments to remember the times in your life that were most meaningful to your walk with God. These are the moments when you first began to sense that God was calling your name for full time vocational service in his Kingdom. So, right now, sit back, take a deep breath, close your eyes, and just think. Go ahead and take the next 10 seconds and reminisce over what God did to bring you to this point in your life.

If you are like me, your mind went back to those three-hour-long altar services at camp, mission trips to Mexico, and powerful experiences with the Holy Spirit in youth group. Or maybe you came to the Lord later in life, and your mind traveled to the moment when God woke you up out of your spiritual sleep, rocked your world, told you to sell your business, and go on the mission field. Whatever your unique story, I'll bet your most meaningful moments were connected to one thing in particular, your experience and involvement in your local church.

Here is how many of you began. This is not an exhaustive list, but maybe you can relate to a few of them.

- You went to youth camp to get away from the house for a week and ended up getting saved and called into pastoral ministry.

- You got involved with the praise team in youth group.

- You volunteered to set up and tear down the chairs for services.

- You did drama, human videos, and skits.

- You and a few friends got together, called yourself a rock band, went on tour, and preached the gospel to all of your tattooed friends.

- You went to South Africa on a mission trip with your church to build an orphanage.

You fill in the blank with your story, but the fact remains, you got involved. You began to invest your time, money, efforts, talent, love, and yes, your passion to your local church, and God used that to speak to your heart about the greater cause of the Kingdom.

Now that you have thought through your personal experiences in times past, I want you to ask yourself this very important question. Do you think you would have been on fire for God back then if you had not personally sacrificed and invested in the Kingdom of God? The answer? Not a chance in this world. There is no way you would have been as passionate for God if you had not placed yourself in a position for God to use you. Then, once you knew the feeling of impacting your generation for Christ, you knew there was nothing else that could ever fulfill you except serving God.

-THE POWER OF PERSONAL INVESTMENT-

If we needed to invest ourselves to kindle a fire for God back then, what makes us think there is any difference now that we are in Christian college? This is the question that I hope to tackle in this chapter.

my story

Not long after I arrived in Springfield, I started getting an itch. This itch had nothing to do with poison ivy. You will all probably feel this way a few weeks after enrollment at your school. You will get the itch to minister. It makes perfect sense to want to go out and get involved somewhere because you just came from an environment where you were needed and appreciated for your services. After the euphoria of new classes, new friends, new town, new restaurants, and new movie theaters wears off, the longing to be needed in a local church will set in again. Getting involved and investing yourself is critical for sustaining your passion for God, yet there must be a balance in this area. There will be a temptation to over work and get too involved too fast. We will talk more about this in chapter 5. But for the purposes of this chapter, I want to highlight the value of appropriately investing yourself into someone else.

Hopefully, you will have chosen a Christian college that will provide a number of opportunities for you to get involved with ministry teams from your campus and point you in the right direction for church involvement. I am sure that you will be able to get plugged into any number of things like a campus praise team, drama team, or traveling ministry team. Many schools will offer Spring Break mission trips, giving you the great chance

to see more of the world. Whatever you decide to do, here are
a few things to keep in mind.

DO'S AND DON'TS

<u>Do something you enjoy.</u> If you can't enjoy your ministry, then why do it?

<u>Do something that will stretch you.</u> If you continue to do things in which you are already proficient, then you will cease to grow.

<u>Do something you have never done before.</u> Stretch your imagination and your experience by going to a country or city that is new to you. God will use these moments to open your eyes to a world much bigger than yourself.

<u>Do something that will develop the gifts God has placed inside you.</u> Paul told Timothy to "fan into flame the gift of God that is inside you…" The gifts that are inside you were placed there for a reason. Do not commit the sin of burying your talents.

<u>Don't do something that is comfortable.</u> Comfortable moments do not provide the means through which we grow and develop. God uses the most uncomfortable moments to mold us into the people we are called to be.

<u>Don't do something just because everyone else is doing it.</u> There may be certain ministries on campus that you will be tempted to join just because they are popular. Be sure to spend time in prayer before committing to a particular ministry.

<u>Don't be led by status;</u> be led by the Holy Spirit.

<u>Don't do something that takes away from your studies.</u> Remember that one of the main reasons you are in a Christian

-THE POWER OF PERSONAL INVESTMENT-

college is to learn and come to a deeper understanding of God's Word. If your involvement begins to cause your grades to fall, consider cutting back a little.

<u>Don't do something that you feel pressured to do.</u> Maybe your group of close friends is all joining a particular church or ministry, and they want you to join as well. Learn now to say the all-important word NO. The word NO is your best friend.

When you begin your freshman year, the opportunities for ministry will begin piling up. Only weeks after I began Christian college, I became involved with a local church leading worship for their college group that met early on Sunday mornings. This was a great way for me to meet other people in college and use the gift that God had given me to lead worship. Soon I became involved with campus praise teams, traveling music groups, and in my sophomore year, I went on a Spring Break mission trip to Guatemala. I became involved with the student government, and through that experience I was able to invest myself into the lives of hundreds of my fellow classmates. I can honestly say that my personal investment played a major role in the preservation and elevation of my passion for God. I believe there would have been no chance for me to complete four years of Christian college with my FIRE intact without having personally invested into the lives of others.

That is the way it was for me. That is the way it was for Elijah.

-CHAPTER 4-

THE MANTLE
OF PERSONAL INVESTMENT

- 1 Kings 19:19 -

"So he departed from there, and found Elisha the son of Shaphat, who was plowing with twelve yoke of oxen before him, and he was with the twelfth. <u>Then Elijah passed by him and threw his mantle on him."</u> (emphasis added)

In verse 16, God told Elijah to go and anoint Elisha as his successor. This was the initiation of one of the greatest personal investments in all of history. The significance of the moment is difficult to grasp at the beginning, but when you dig a little deeper you realize that Elijah changed the destiny of this young farmer by starting a relationship geared for purpose. Because Elijah obeyed God and took the time to throw his mantle on Elisha, the possibility was provided that one day Elisha would grow up to reach his full potential. The Bible records that Elisha immediately began to follow and serve the prophet. There are not many details given to us about his daily rituals or duties, but we are given a clue in 2 Kings 3:11. It says, *"...Elisha the son of Shaphat is here, who poured water on the hands of Elijah."* We can know from this verse that Elisha walked closely with Elijah and served him in ways that may or may not seem significant, but the reality is that Elisha was being taught two of the most important lessons of ministry: self-denial and service.

Being the right hand man of the prophet of God was anything but comfortable. Being his servant was hard work, earned little pay, and I would imagine little self gratification. There was not a lot of acclaim that came with the position, but the world may have never known one of the greatest leaders of all time had not Elijah taken the time to pour himself into Elisha.

What if Elijah had never believed in the importance of personal investment? How would the course of history have been changed if Elijah had never thrown the mantle? If Elijah had not taken the time to throw his mantle, people would have died when they otherwise would have lived. People would have starved when they otherwise would have been fed. People would have been sick when they otherwise would have been healed. The miraculous was reproduced in Elisha. Because of the mantle of mentorship, thousands more encountered the miraculous as well.

- Bringing It Home -

Do you have someone right now, a younger student at school or young person at your church, into whom you are currently pouring your spirit of excellence and passion for prayer? Are you leading a small group or a Bible study on campus or in your church? Are you involved? Have you thrown your mantle? If the answer is no, then you are on a fast track to losing the very heart of what you were called to do. Consider this. Who will not be impacted by the love and Gospel of Jesus Christ if you don't throw your mantle? Think of all the people who will not be fed, healed, saved, and brought back to life if you do not throw the mantle.

Being a mentor or a teacher is not easy or convenient. This life-shaping activity will not always fit perfectly into your schedule. Having a protégée will not be a comfortable experience. But we all need to wake up and understand that ministry is rarely comfortable, convenient, or compact. Ministry is often simply doing what we know to be the right thing, in this case, raising up our successors and replacements. We are called to throw the mantle.

Is throwing the mantle hard work? Absolutely. Without a doubt reproducing ourselves will be one of the most challenging things we'll ever do, if we do it right. But the reward will far outweigh the difficulty. The outcome of throwing the mantle will be the raising up of the next generation of those who will carry on the high calling of proclaiming the word of God. There is no greater honor in this world.

You may be feeling down, depressed, or like you are all alone in your struggles. You might be having one of the world's biggest pity parties. You might be at your wit's end. If that is the case, then you are in good company. Elijah felt that way in the verses immediately preceding the call of Elisha. Here is an interesting thought. What did God do to rekindle the fire and passion of Elijah? He told him to THROW THE MANTLE.

- A quick thought on Elisha's Fire -

Elisha would not have possessed his skill sets, abilities, talents, wisdom, understanding, knowledge, and yes...FIRE without a mentor, someone who took the time to personally invest into him. Not only is mentoring someone else vital to your personal development, but you must also have someone older and wiser than you pouring themselves into your life. Elisha did not have just anyone as his spiritual mentor. He had the right person at the right time with the right qualifications.

-THE POWER OF PERSONAL INVESTMENT-

There are at least three things we need to consider when bringing ourselves under an authority figure for the purpose of mentorship and accountability.

<u>1. Right Person:</u> As we read through this account in 1 Kings 19, we see that Elisha did not pick Elijah. Elijah chose Elisha. This seems to be the case many times throughout scripture, from Moses to Jesus. God divinely inspired leaders to pick their disciples. Many times in Christian circles, having a "mentor" or an "accountability partner" becomes little more than a trend. It can be just another thing to check off the spiritual to do list. Don't allow that to happen in your life. Pray and ask God for wisdom as he brings you and the right mentor together.

<u>2. Right Time:</u> It has been said that timing is everything, and this certainly rings true as it relates to the mentorship process. As it says in Ecclesiastes 3:1, *"There is a time for everything, and a season for every activity under heaven."* The mentorship process should not be something that is forced. It must be something that flows smoothly as God's hand guides the relationship to a proper beginning and a proper end. Pray and ask God to keep you from pushing the issue to a premature beginning. God will bring you and your mentor together at the right time as you trust in him. Philippians 4:6 encourages us, *"Do not be anxious about anything, but in everything, by prayer and petition, with thanksgiving, present your requests to God."*

<u>3. Right Qualifications:</u> Elijah did not approach Elisha at the beginning of his ministry. There was a season of proving that took place in Elijah's life before God brought him to Elisha. He had already prophesied that there would be no rain and there was none. He had helped the widow at Zarephath.

-CHAPTER 4-

He had raised the dead, confronted kings, and defeated false prophets by the power of Almighty God. All of this before he came into Elisha's life. This gives us a clue as to who we should allow into our lives as mentors. It should be seasoned men and women of God who have proven themselves to be of godly character and knowledge. They will have the proper credentials and experience to back up what they say and teach. We cannot afford to let a novice into our lives. If we do, we will get novice results.

Remember what it tells us in James 3:1: *"Not many of you should presume to be teachers, my brothers, because you know that we who teach will be judged more strictly."*

Two of the greatest practices for keeping your passion for God while in Christian college are (1) investing yourself into someone else AND (2) having the right person invest into you.

JOURNAL & DISCUSS

1. How are you currently involved in ministry, either on campus or in a local church?

_____

_____

_____

_____

2. Who is currently investing into you (i.e. a pastor, campus pastor, youth pastor, professor)?

_____

_____

_____

_____

3. What are some strategies that you could put in place to help you to continue in these relationships?

_____

_____

_____

_____

Other Thoughts or Comments:

_____

_____

_____

_____

_____

_____

PART II

KEEPING YOUR FIRE FOR GOD

CHAPTER 5
RESISTING TEMPTATION

One very cool evening in December of 2003, I was lying in bed staring up at a ceiling on the 9th floor of a skyscraper in the middle of Santiago, Chile. My wife Sara is from the country of Chile, and I went there to spend Christmas with her family for one major reason. Obviously at the time Sara was not yet my wife, and I wanted to do the proper thing and ask her father's permission before I popped the big question. The sound of the traffic eight floors below was making me drowsy, but the many thoughts that were rushing through my mind were keeping me awake. "What will her father say?" I thought. I wondered if he would be happy for us. I wondered if I would have the courage to face him the next day. (In the end, everything in that department went great. As I am writing this chapter, Sara and I have been married 4 years, and we are expecting our first baby girl.) Asking for Sara's hand in marriage was not the only thought that was flooding my mind that night in Santiago. I was also dreaming and contemplating the future of our ministry together. Where would we be? What would God do through us as a couple? When would God launch us into our moments of destiny? Lurking inside this particular series of thoughts were the seeds to some of the greatest moments of temptation that I would ever face at Christian college.

Anyone who really knows me will tell you that I would rather be preaching than doing anything else in this world. If I had to make a choice between eating and preaching, I would be a much skinnier person today. Like the prophet Jeremiah, the word of God is like a fire shut up in my bones, and I cannot help wanting to deliver the life-giving, life-shaping message of the Gospel of Jesus Christ. But like everything else in this world, there is a proper time and a season for everything. That includes the timing of our launch into full-time ministry.

Remembering that night in Santiago is not hard for me. The memory is so vividly imprinted on my mind that I can still hear the car horns blaring, the wind blowing through the balcony door, and the way the room seemed to shift with the moonlight. The reason for my good memory is because I was lying there thinking of a way that I could shortcut the journey of Christian college. Like a crying two year old in the middle of a department store, I was whining, "I WANNA BE IN MINISTRY NOW! I WANT IT NOW, NOW, NOW!" So I came up with a plan. What I did next was one of the greatest failures of my entire college career, but God used this failure to teach me an invaluable lesson. Had the Lord not intervened through some very trusted people in my life, I fear that I would have personally snuffed out the flame of my own passion by the end of the spring semester.

Very soon after I returned from my trip to Chile during Christmas break, I contacted a friend of mine that I had met at CBC. John (not his real name) was the same age as I, but he was already the pastor of his own church. After calling him on the phone and catching up on what we did over the break, I asked him if he currently had a youth pastor. He said no and was delighted to speak with me about potentially coming on staff with him. I could not have been more excited about the possibility of being on paid staff at a church and working with a good friend of mine. I know that on the outset this may not sound like such a bad idea, but allow me to describe for you the circumstances surrounding this seemingly great opportunity.

Just because a church is a great church with a great pastor and great people doesn't necessarily mean that God is calling you to be a part of that particular work. You see, the location of the church was over three hours away from school. For me to be able to be a part of this wonderful ministry I would have to commute there every Saturday, stay the night, and return Sunday evening. There would be times when I would have had to make the commute for special occasions and events, not to mention the extreme difficultly of being available for my students if they needed me for whatever reason. If I had been thinking clearly and listening to some very wise loved ones, I would have seen that this ministry opportunity would be an added stress on my studies and distract me from my main purpose, which was preparing for ministry. But did I listen to them? No! And what happened next was an even greater hardship.

With more enthusiasm than I had ever shown before, I happily accepted the position as youth pastor at this wonderful church. All the while my fiancé, my parents, my future in-laws, and other family members were urging me to wait on God's timing, but I refused to listen. In a last ditch effort to get my eyes to see the folly of my ways, God spoke through a wise elderly woman in a chapel service the Wednesday before I was about to be introduced to the congregation. You might be able to guess what she spoke on that morning. Her topic discussed the importance of waiting on God to release you into ministry. God was trying everything he could to get my attention, but I hardened my heart to the good judgment of friends, family, and even God. And I reaped the consequences.

Soon the time came for me to be introduced to the congregation as the new youth pastor. I drove the more than three hours to the church, dressed in my best suit and tie, smiling from ear to ear. My friend John took the platform and energetically introduced me. Everyone applauded as I came to greet the crowd. I gave a passionate speech about how I desired to reach the youth of that city and laid out a vision for how I planned to do just that. After the service, everyone was so happy that I was there, and they even threw me a welcoming dinner to make me feel right at home. Everything was going perfectly, that is until the long ride home.

On the way home, God made it overwhelmingly clear that I was walking in disobedience. I tried everything I could to justify my actions. I argued with God that I could handle the responsibility of being in ministry and being in school. Debating with the Lord has never worked out for me in the past, but still, I persisted in this futile exercise. In the end, I gave in, and what I had to do next was among the most painful experiences of my life up until that point. I knew I had to come clean and tell John that I could not continue as his youth pastor. I may have set a new world record for the shortest time ever spent at a ministry, but I did what I had to do. I made the call, and trust me: you never want to have to make a call like that one.

-RESISTING TEMPTATION-

The consequences for my actions were severe. Number one, I put John in a very uncomfortable position with his congregation. Here he was pledging his support for me one Sunday and the very next he had to tell them that I would not continue as youth pastor. Number two, my friendship with John was never the same. He and I did make amends, but we never made it back to the level of camaraderie that we once had. Number three, I put myself through some very avoidable and unneeded embarrassment. I know I made the right choice in ending this ministry opportunity as soon as I could, but there was no reason for me to have had to go through this in the first place if I had just listened to what God was trying to tell me in the beginning.

I learned a hard lesson during that spring of 2004, a lesson that I will not soon forget. The timing of the Lord is everything in ministry, and allowing yourself to become overwhelmed with ministry responsibilities during Christian college will become one of the quickest ways for you to lose your fire and passion for God. I praise God that I did the right thing in the end. Learn from my mistake and save yourself the pain and embarrassment of backtracking. Listen to the voice of the Lord and realize that in his time he will release you. As I mentioned in chapter 4, you should be involved in appropriate levels of ministry during your time of preparation. Please do not confuse that, however, with what I am talking about here. To keep your fire through Christian college you must resist the temptation of jumping ahead of God's perfect timing to be released into full- time vocational ministry.

This was true for me. This was true for Joseph.

-CHAPTER 5-

Aggressively Resisting Temptation:
DON'T WALK, RUN
- Genesis 39:6-8 & 12 -

"...Now Joseph was well-built and handsome, and after a while his master's wife took notice of Joseph and said, "Come to bed with me!" But he refused..." She caught him by his cloak and said, "Come to bed with me!" But he left his cloak in her hand and ran out of the house." (emphasis added)

There is no doubt that Joseph was an amazing leader and that his life was marked by a divine providence that strategically placed him in positions of great influence. However, he did not come to this level of leadership by way of an easy road. His road was accentuated with tragedy, despair, and disappointment. He was hated and mocked by his brothers, thrown into a pit, sold into slavery, and taken to a foreign land. Before he was treated so harshly by the ones closest to him, he was given a vision from the Lord of his future greatness. He knew he was to be someone great, and at the young age of seventeen the possibilities seemed endless. But all of that changed one day without any warning or notice. All of his hopes were dashed, and his dreams were destroyed.

Often though, on the hard and difficult roads, we actually find the perfect environments in which God can mold and shape us into the people we are called to be. Genesis 50:20 states, *"You intended to harm me, but God intended it for good to accomplish what is now being done, the saving of many lives"*. This is an incredible account to read through again and watch how the Lord continued to prosper Joseph, promoting him to places of almost absolute authority. It didn't matter where he was, in Potiphar's house or in the jail house, people trusted Joseph and paid no attention to anything under Joseph's care, because the LORD was with Joseph and gave him success in whatever he did (Gen. 39:23). The million-dollar question is, "Why did God see fit to promote Joseph the way that He did?" What made Joseph so special? There must have been something unique about Joseph's character that pleased God, and if so, what was it? I believe that verses 8 and 12 tell us everything that we need to know. He refused and ran from temptation. He didn't just passively walk away from it. He refused and ran.

Joseph was strong and in great shape after years of hard work in the fields as a boy and under his master's charge as a slave. The Bible describes him as well built and handsome. Joseph was in his physical prime, and there is no doubt that his hormones were raging within him like any other young man at that age. Still, there was something burning deep inside of him that caused him to walk upright and just before the Lord and his master Potiphar. There was a fire and passion for the Lord in his gut that gave him the ability to walk with character and integrity even in the face of daily temptation. Verse 10 says, *"And though she spoke to Joseph day after day, he <u>refused</u> to go to bed with her or even be with her"* (emphasis added). Day after day temptation came, and to a young man there are few temptations greater than this kind. Still, in the midst of this almost impossible situation, Joseph remained pure. How? He was an aggressive resister of temptation!

-CHAPTER 5-

- Bringing It Home -

The hero of this story gives us such an incredible example of how we should handle temptation. Oh how I wish I had applied this lesson to my life in the spring of '04, but there is no reason why you can't learn from my failure AND Joseph's success. There is no reason why you can't be an aggressive resister of temptation because I know that my God is more than able to provide for you a way of escape from every temptation you face (I Cor. 10:13)...especially the temptation to accept a ministry position before his time.

Consider for a moment what kind of leader Joseph would have been if he had sidestepped his time of preparation. He received his calling at the age of seventeen. What if he said at that moment, "I think I will just travel to Egypt, walk right up to Pharaoh, relay to him my dreams of greatness, and tell him that I am supposed to be the second in command of all the land. I will tell you exactly what would have happened. His ambitions would have killed him! If not literally, his hopes of ever reaching his purpose would have been killed. We must travel the road of preparation if we ever hope to arrive at our destiny. THERE ARE NO SHORTCUTS. The road is not an easy one, but both necessary AND worth the journey.

-A Word To The Wise-

Offers May Come, Be Ready: If you are in Christian college, there may be people who will make offers, but you can't afford to be shortsighted. Realize that there will ALWAYS be other offers, but the season of preparation must be seen through to the end first.

-RESISTING TEMPTATION-

Be Aggressive: Don't even flirt with the idea of shortcutting your time at Christian college. Don't just resist the temptation passively. RUN from the temptation. Follow our hero's example and save yourself the pain and embarrassment that I faced.

If you can be the type of person who is aggressive in your understanding of resisting the temptation to leave Christian college prematurely, then you are well on your way to not only keeping your passion for God intact, but also having what's necessary for success in the ministry for the long haul. Take this time in your life to learn one of the greatest lessons that any Christian can learn: we must always walk in the perfect timing of the Lord. Only then can we have what's necessary to reach our destiny.

JOURNAL & DISCUSS

Could you relate with my personal story in any way? If so, what could you do to keep yourself from falling into the same trap that I did?

_____

_____

_____

_____

How well do you listen when God is trying to get your attention and warn you about something?

_____

_____

_____

_____

How do you aggressively resist temptation?

_____

_____

_____

_____

Other Thoughts or Comments:

_____

_____

_____

_____

CHAPTER 6
NEVER SELL OUT

my story

One of the most rewarding things that I did during college was joining a traveling musical group. I played the acoustic guitar and was honored to be able to use my gift and love of music during my school years. We traveled a lot and covered several different states leading worship and performing in many different churches during breaks and throughout the summer months. This experience added fuel to my fire for God because it kept me fresh and connected with ministry in a local church setting. However, if you have ever dealt with musicians and performers, then you know that there can be many moments of drama and attitude. Allow me to share with you one such incident.

Traveling several hours to our destination was a normal thing for us, but this time we only had to travel a couple of hours to our next ministry opportunity. This church was a beautiful little community church with probably less than 150 people in attendance. The pastor was a kind man who had been there for many years. He loved the people, and the people loved him. The sanctuary was small with rows of old, dark, wooden pews, old carpet, wooden paneling halfway up the walls, and a stage full of old, used musical equipment complete with a piano and an organ. I guess by now you are getting the picture that this church looked and felt old, because it was old. But the people were kind, they loved the Lord, and they were very appreciative of our ministry. I will never forget what happened as we walked into the sanctuary to begin setting up.

One of the musicians and I walked in at the same time carrying our equipment, and I looked over at him and noticed that he had a look of utter disgust on his face. He looked over at me with a smug little smirk and said, "Who could ever lead worship in a place like this every week? I could never take a ministry position in a place like this." I had to draw on all of my strength to stay in control and not blow up on this guy. I wanted to give him a piece of my mind. However, God gave me grace in that moment, and I just ignored him. I am just happy that no one else heard him say those awful words.

Months later, our group was invited to lead worship and perform at a very large and prestigious church. This was a church where several thousand people were in weekly attendance. The sanctuary was modern, complete with lights, cameras, and all the new musical equipment you could ever dream of having. Truthfully, the facility was incredible and any minister would be blessed to be in a place like that, but is that what following Christ in ministry is really all about? You can probably guess what happened next. This same friend of mine and I were walking in together to begin setting up our equipment. He walked in the door, put his hands on his hips, looked around, nodded his head, and said these words: "Now this is the kind of church that I am going to work for when

I graduate." I couldn't believe my ears. Was it really the buildings and the equipment and the prestige that were guiding my friend's decisions? What about the leading of the Holy Spirit? Doesn't he get a say in where we go in ministry after graduation?

These questions and more began to race through my mind. I just shook my head in utter amazement at my friend's cavalier attitude and ignored him. I honestly felt sorry for him, but I never forgot those moments. I never forgot my friend's words. I never forgot his attitude, and I made an inner vow then and there that I would never sell out or bypass the leading of the Lord for the glamour of a "big" ministry.

Fast-forward the clock four years, and I am now approaching graduation. My schedule had become quite hectic by this time. I had a part-time job at the National Headquarters of the Assemblies of God. I had a part-time youth pastor position in a local church. I was carrying the load of 17 credit hours in school, and I was (and still am) a happily married man. You could say I had a full schedule, but the Lord was gracious and helped me to end my time at Christian college with some amount of success. Along with success, however, came moments of temptation to sell out. Allow me to explain because one of my biggest opportunities for selling out was about to take place.

I was working in a local church at the time as their part-time youth pastor. I must say that working at that church was one of the best experiences of my life. God allowed me to work under an amazing pastor and minister to some of the most awesome kids in the whole world. But that isn't the whole story. My wife and I accepted the position of part-time youth pastors at this church at the beginning of our junior year in college. My pastor asked me to make a commitment to him that I would be there for at least three years before considering another ministry position. I gave him my word that I would continue on as youth pastor for three years, and I take that very seriously. In ministry, all you have is your word. Without that, you have nothing.

Life went on normally for about a year and a half until one day I received a phone call while I was working my other job at the National Headquarters. Someone was letting me know about a fast-growing church in their area that needed a youth pastor. They recommended that I look into it. Anyone would have been blessed to pursue that opportunity, but there was one problem...I had given my word to my pastor. I was committed for three years, so I declined to look into that church. This person persisted and informed me that these types of chances only come once in a lifetime and that I was crazy not to at least look into it. I told this person that there was something more important to me than working in a big church, and that was my word. I gave my word to my pastor, and really, that is all that mattered. I said no, and that was that. Here is how the story ends.

Not long after that conversation, my pastor began feeling led of the Lord to pursue other opportunities elsewhere in ministry. He brought me into his office and sat me down to let me know of his decision. He released me to begin looking into other ministry options if I wanted. Out of respect for him, and out of my respect for the future pastor of the church, I willingly submitted my resignation and began to pray and seek God for direction. Only a few months later, God opened the door for us to come on staff at a wonderful church as full-time youth pastors in the great state of Texas. We know that the Lord directed us here, and we are thrilled to see the results of the ministry God has given us to fulfill.

Was making the decision to just shrug off the idea of working in a large and growing church that was close to family and friends easy? NO!!! All I had to do was go back on my word to my pastor, and I could climb the church corporate ladder. All I had to do was compromise the most important thing I had (my word), and I could achieve "ministry success." All I had to do to really be somebody was sell out. But I remembered those words that my friend spewed from his mouth when we walked into that little church with dark pews and old equipment. "How could anyone work in a place like this?" I never want to become someone who would be willing to sell out something as important as my word just for a "better" venue.

Let me clarify something before I go any further. I do not think that working in a large church means you have sold out. I currently work in a fairly large church, and I know that I am exactly where God has called me to be. But coming to the place where you would be willing to sell out the most important things to be at a larger and more prestigious church is the issue. God has an inheritance for us. He has a calling for us to fulfill, and he has a very specific geographical location in which we need to fulfill it. We cannot sell out that inheritance for glamour and prestige. Staying true to who you are and to your principles is how you keep your fire burning white-hot.

This was true for me. This was true for Naboth.

-CHAPTER 6-

Naboth Resolved: NEVER SELL OUT
- 1 Kings 21:2 -
"Ahab said to Naboth, "Let me have your vineyard to use for a vegetable garden, since it is close to my palace. In exchange I will give you a better vineyard or, if you prefer, I will pay you whatever it is worth.""

- 1 Kings 21:3 -
"But Naboth replied, "The LORD forbid that I should give you the inheritance of my fathers.""

There will always be people throughout your career who will approach you and offer you something in exchange for the one thing you have that is infinitely more valuable, your word. There will always be times in school and ministry when the "grass will seem greener on the other side." They will come smiling, excited, passionate, and ready to pay out, but before you sell out, you must evaluate what is truly your most prized possession. Once your promises are broken, once your word is lost, it is lost forever. At the very best, it is damaged forever. When those offers come at just the wrong moments, after we have pledged ourselves elsewhere, what do we do? To whom can we look to help us navigate these confusing waters? Enter Naboth.

We do not know a whole lot about Naboth. He is only mentioned a few times in the Bible, but what we do know about him is very interesting. I have always found his account to be inspiring. At first glance, his story might seem to be a trivial tail about a stubborn man who refused to sell his property, and in

55

the end his resolve got him killed. But a secondary look into the life of Naboth will prove to be eternally rewarding.

Of one thing we can be certain: he was a man of great conviction. He was willing to stand up to the most ruthless and powerful man in the land. In the face of King Ahab's demand for his property, Naboth was unwilling to compromise. He was unwilling to sell out. Chapter 21 of 1 Kings is not a very long chapter, but it has a lot to say to us regarding what is most important in life.

"Naboth said, "The LORD forbid that I should give you the inheritance of my fathers."" You see, his name was wrapped up in that land. It had been in his family for generations, and now someone was coming who wanted it. In essence, Naboth would be giving up his name and the names of all of those who came before him. King Ahab was asking to erase Naboth's name from that land and put his name on it. That was out of the question for Naboth. He realized the importance of his name, and he wasn't going to sell out. Even if that meant getting a better vineyard or being paid a certain amount of money, he would never sell his name.

Look at what verse 2 says. *"Ahab said to Naboth, "Let me have your vineyard to use for a vegetable garden, since it is close to my palace.""* A vegetable garden? What? You mean Ahab did not want to use it for the purpose for which it was intended? He wanted to change it? He wanted to make it into something else, something that fit his mold? That's right folks! If the "king" is making an offer you can't refuse, he probably has other motives.

That land had a purpose. It was meant to be a vineyard,

yet Ahab doesn't seem to care about what it was meant to be. He had his own ulterior motives. Those who are willing to ask you to compromise what's most important in life usually do. If someone is willing to cut corners and try to tempt you out of a situation that you know you are supposed to be in, then let that be a red flag to you that you may have an Ahab on your hands who wants to take your vineyard and make a vegetable garden out of it.

- Bringing It Home -

I once met a man who was part of a local Teen Challenge group in the city in which I minister. He was a wonderful man who knew the Lord and was getting his once mixed up life put back together. One day unexpectedly his past came back to haunt him. His life before he came to Christ was polluted with drugs and gambling. He did whatever he could to nurse these habits along, including accepting drugs from drug dealers without giving payment. All he used to care about was getting the quick fix, even if it meant having to pay them back at a later time.

Months had passed since he had been on any kind of drug or placed any bets, but on this unforgiving day he got a knock on the door from some uninvited guests. The drug dealer's muscle showed up demanding money and threatened to take the payment from his flesh. My friend explained to them that he no longer lived that life, but because he wanted to protect his family and himself, he paid the debt. The men left and no one was hurt. Thank God!

That story could have ended a lot differently, and I thank

God that everything turned out okay. Our story may not turn out so nicely if we are willing to take from the "spiritual loan sharks." If we are willing to compromise and take the quick money, the quick promotion, the quick rise up the political ladder, one day the ones who put us where we are will come to collect on their loan. They will come knocking at the door unexpectedly and demand what is rightfully theirs. And when that happens, the only thing left for you to do will be to dig your pit of compromise even deeper.

When God promotes, however, a much different story unfolds. Look at what Proverbs 10:22 says:

> *"The blessing of the LORD, it maketh rich, and he addeth no sorrow with it."*

God's way is a much better way because his way provides us with the ability to rise on our character and integrity, not our political savvy.

The next time someone comes along and makes you an offer on your name and your word, follow the example of Naboth and refuse to have a price tag on what's most important. I am sure you have heard the phrase, "Everyone has a price." But there are some things that can never have a price, and one of them is your fire for God. Keep your fire for God burning through your Christian college experience and your ministry, and say along with the hero of our story, "The LORD forbid that I should give you the inheritance of my fathers." NEVER SELL OUT!

JOURNAL & DISCUSS

How did it make you feel when you read how my friend reacted differently to the "small church" as opposed to the "glamorous church"?

_____

_____

_____

_____

How well do you keep your word when it is given? Is backing out on a promise an option for you? When is it okay, in your opinion, to go back on your word?

_____

_____

_____

_____

Take a minute to list 5-7 character qualities that you admire most in leaders.

_____

_____

_____

_____

_____

_____

_____

CHAPTER 7
WE ARE NOT GODS

Ninety thousand screaming fans poured into a soccer stadium in South America one afternoon in 1987 for one reason: to hear and see the great evangelist from the U.S. The arena was packed and the atmosphere was the same as that of a championship game as the man of God delivered his message of hope and salvation. The evening rally began with a very unique occurrence.

All day long local missionaries and pastors had hosted the evangelist and his entourage of helpers. On occasion, in this particular South American country, a star athlete or the MVP of the game would take what's called a "victory lap" around the quarter mile track of the stadium to allow the crowd to show their honor and appreciation for the champion.

As the evangelist entered the stadium, the applause mounted and he raised both hands high. It took him almost 15 minutes to circle the stadium track, allowing the ninety thousand people to pour their adoration and praise on him instead of on the ONE who gave him his many talents. Afterwards a missionary leader commented to some of his colleagues that this should have been a red flag to everyone who knew or was associated with the evangelist.

It wasn't too long after that moment that the internationally known speaker and minister had a terrible moral failure, which not only destroyed his passion for God and ministry but also delivered a major blow to the Body of Christ worldwide.

If there was one guiding principle that I could leave you with in this final chapter it would be this: Never believe your own press. Never believe that you have somehow reached the point of "ministry success" and miraculously climbed the ladder to its highest rung. Many people, from actors to religious leaders from around the world have said this, and it is so true. In those pivotal times that we begin to think that we have achieved a level of celebrity, we have stepped over an unforeseeable line into an area called pride. And that, my friends, is not only one of the quickest ways to lose your fire for God, but also put you on a fast track to total ministry failure.

The Bible reiterates the same thing but in a different way in Proverbs 16:18 when it says, "Pride goes before destruction, a haughty spirit before a fall." If you want to successfully complete Christian college with your passion intact, then learn this lesson now because this lesson, as well as the others in this book, will keep you balanced throughout your years of ministry. Learn that there is always someone else to whom you should give the credit. Even if the possibility existed to take credit for all the work, you would still need to give credit to the Lord Jesus Christ for gifting you and enabling you to achieve your results. The results are always in the Father's hands.

1 Corinthians 3:7 says, *"So then neither he who plants is anything, nor he who waters, but God who gives the increase."*

-WE ARE NOT GODS-

No matter what situation we find ourselves in, whether we are the planter or the person who waters, we can do nothing apart from the help of someone else.

My Christian college experience was one of the best experiences of my life. It helped me in more ways than I could ever list because there God formed, shaped, molded, and refined me into the minister I am today. But can I honestly say that I didn't have help along the way? Absolutely not! I have made it a practice to give credit where credit is due, and this situation is no different. My professors, teachers, pastors, friends, and most of all, my wife, all played a major role in my quest to reach the finish line. I am not trying to down play our own responsibility of working hard, studying, and performing with excellence in all that we do. All I am trying to say is that we don't get anywhere in life alone. If we think we achieve greatness by ourselves or by our own merit, we are setting ourselves up for the biggest fall of our lives. Unfortunately, like the evangelist in our story, the fall will affect more lives than you can imagine. If we expect to continue through Christian college and beyond with our hearts on fire for the ONE who gave his life for us, then we must always point back and give credit to others and most of all to Jesus Christ.

This was true for the evangelist. This was true for me. This was true for Paul and Barnabas.

-CHAPTER 7-

Paul & Barnabas Reflected: WE ARE NOT GODS!
- Acts 14:11-15 -

"When the crowd saw what Paul had done, they shouted in the Lycaonian language, "The gods have come down to us in human form!" Barnabas they called Zeus, and Paul they called Hermes because he was the chief speaker. The priest of Zeus, whose temple was just outside the city, brought bulls and wreaths to the city gates because he and the crowd wanted to offer sacrifices to them.

But when the apostles Barnabas and Paul heard of this, they tore their clothes and rushed out into the crowd, shouting: Men, why are you doing this? We too are only men, human like you. We are bringing you good news, telling you to turn from these worthless things to the living God, who made heaven and earth and sea and everything in them."

Paul and Barnabas had traveled to the polytheistic city of Lystra to continue their first tour of missionary work. As anyone entered this city a temple to the god Zeus would have greeted them along with a statue of Hermes, the chief speaker for Zeus. This was a very superstitious city that was filled with idol worship and cultic practices, and they believed that Zeus was the creator and sustainer of the entire universe, causing the changing of the seasons. Paul and Barnabas knew that this was a place that desperately needed the Gospel of Jesus Christ, and so they began to evangelize and speak the good news. A man who had been crippled from birth was listening to Paul speak. Paul took notice of this unfortunate man and prayed that God would heal him of his infirmity. Immediately the man was made whole, and that is when everything spiraled out of control.

When the people there saw the great miracle that had been worked through Paul, they began to associate him with their god Hermes. To them, Paul seemed to be speaking on behalf of his companion Barnabas, so they called Barnabas Zeus. The people were amazed at this wonder that had been worked in their midst. They had never experienced anything so real and tangible in their lives, so they simply assumed that this must be the work of their gods. The people simply had no other frame of reference for what had transpired in front of them, so they identified Paul and Barnabas as divine beings sent to them in human likeness.

As the scene continues to unfold, the heroes of our story notice that the priest from the temple of Zeus had brought out sacrifices to be offered to them. This gave Paul and Barnabas the much needed opportunity that they had been looking for to point to the real Creator and Sustainer of life: Almighty God. At once Paul and Barnabas arrested their attention and stopped them from continuing down this unfruitful path. They reflected all credit to Almighty God, and explained to them that he is the one true and living God who has created everything in heaven and earth. They continued to show them that their worship of idols and gods made by man's hands was pointless when they could serve a living God. Even in the face of all of this, the Bible tells us that the apostles were scarcely able to stop the people from offering sacrifices to them.

-CHAPTER 7-

- Bringing It Home -

If ever Paul and Barnabas were looking for an opportunity to set themselves up as superstars, this would have been it. The people literally wanted to worship them as divine and would have served Paul and Barnabas as their masters. However, in the midst of this great temptation, they quickly found within themselves the ability to point back to God, the Giver of their abilities. When you think about the potential of what they could have done and how they could have used that moment to manipulate the people of Lystra, Paul and Barnabas overcame one of the most difficult temptations ever faced by a minister of the Gospel. That is the temptation to glorify one's self and to set up our own kingdom. Unfortunately, many men and women today have allowed their kingdom to take the place of THE Kingdom in their lives. What can we do to make sure that doesn't happen to us? We must follow the example of Paul and Barnabas.

When someone wants to set you up on a pedestal, just follow these simple steps.

I. Immediately Get Their Attention. It says in verse 14, *"But when the apostles Barnabas and Paul heard of this, they tore their clothes and rushed out into the crowd, shouting."* They didn't savor the moment and talk among themselves wondering what living in Lystra forever as gods in the flesh would be like. They didn't wait around to see exactly how far the people would go with their sacrifices. They didn't even wait to see what their new homes and pay would be if they spent the rest of their days serving in the Temple of Zeus. They didn't waste one moment or give the devil an opportunity to tempt them with the praise of men. They immediately got the people's attention to set the record straight. When people start to raise you up on a pedestal, you can't waste one moment. If you do, the devil will gain ground. The longer you wait, the harder the decision will be to stop people from praising you.

II. Remind Them And Yourself About Who You Really Are.
Verse 15 says, *"Men, why are you doing this? We too are only men, human like you..."* We need to realize that we are just human. What can we really do to save someone's soul? What can we really do in the performance of miracles, signs, and wonders? Can we cause the lame to walk or the blind to see? Can we raise the dead? Can we grant forgiveness for a life of sin and set people free from the bondages of the devil? No. We can do nothing of eternal value apart from the power of the Holy Spirit. We can do nothing apart from God, and in those times we lose sight of that fact that our fire and passion for God is beginning to die. Never forget that we are simply human beings. We are not divine.

III. Give Credit Where It Is Due.
Continuing on in verse 15 it says, *"We are bringing you good news, telling you to turn from these worthless things to the living God, who made heaven and earth and sea and everything in them."* Once they gained their attention and reminded the people and themselves that they were simply human, they

redirected the praise and credit to the only ONE who is worthy of it. God created the universe and everything in it. God gave us life and health and the abilities we have. God is the one who empowers us and places specific gifts and talents in our lives to be used for his glory. No matter how you slice it, the credit belongs squarely on the shoulders of Christ Jesus our Lord.

When someone pays you a compliment, there is nothing wrong with saying, "thank you." When people tell you, "good job" or give you an accolade or two, it is not an evil thing. The problems begin when we start expecting the compliments and accolades. If we cannot be a part of what God is doing without someone saying "good job" or "that was an incredible sermon," then we need to do a serious heart check.

Christian college will present you with many opportunities to excel and develop your skills. While you are learning the ins and outs of preaching, singing, writing, and leading, learn one of the most overlooked skills there is among ministers today: how to gracefully accept praise and reflect it back to the ONE who deserves it. If we do not learn this skill my friends, one day we will find ourselves face to face with our own pride, and it will not only impact our passion for God but other's also.

Never believe your own press. Pass the word.

JOURNAL & DISCUSS

Have you ever been at a place in your life when you began to "believe your own press"? If so, how did you overcome those moments of pride?

_____

_____

_____

_____

How well do you receive compliments? What do you normally do when someone pays you a compliment or two?

_____

_____

_____

_____

What are some creative ways that you have found to reflect praise back to God and give credit to others for the help that they have provided along the way?

_____

_____

_____

_____

_____

CONCLUSION

TRIED BY FIRE

- Proverbs 17:3 -

"The fining pot is for silver, and the furnace for gold: but the LORD trieth the hearts."

Not far from Springfield, Missouri, lies the small town of Branson. This little place became a frequent get-away spot for many of us because we enjoyed going to watch one of its many shows, visiting the IMAX movie theater, or my personal favorite, riding the rides at the local theme park. The reason I enjoyed the theme park so much was because not only did it have rides, it also had a seemingly innumerable amount of arts and crafts exhibits. My favorite exhibit to watch was glassblowing.

Talented artists would take molten glass and create some of the most beautiful works of art I have ever seen. The exhilarating part about this particular show was the fact that they would walk you through every part of the process and show you how each item was created. One of the first things I noticed as I walked into the rustic cabin which housed the glass art was the furnace. This is the place where the glass is prepared and purified so that it can be molded into the masterpiece that its creator wants it to be. The glass is repeatedly passed through thousands of degrees of heat so that every impurity can be removed, and it can become soft enough to craft. Only after being tried by fire could the glass become what it was meant to be.

Allow me to introduce you to just one of the furnaces that you will be put through repeatedly during Christian college, and I want to warn you now not to be blindsided by its effects.

I wish someone had told me as a freshman about this crucible, because honestly, I didn't see it coming. Inside the heat of this refinery I was prepared, purified, and challenged more than I ever had been in my entire life. This is the crucible of the classroom.

I warn you now, do not underestimate the power of the classroom. What are you going to do when you step into the room and your professor challenges almost everything that you have ever believed or understood about the Bible? What are you going to do when you completely and utterly disagree with the lecture that is debunking all of your preconceived notions about theology or doctrine? How are you going to handle the situation when you feel like everything you once knew isn't accurate at all? The crucible of the classroom will get hot, real hot, and you will be faced with a choice. Do you allow the fire to refine your understanding about life and Scripture, or do you run from the heat and never become the masterpiece your Creator intended for you to be?

my story

My freshman year I stepped into my first theology class with a lot of confidence. After all, I had grown up in a pastor's home. I had been in church my entire life, and I was feeling like I knew a little something about Scripture. Then I stepped into the fire, and the next thing I experienced was the revelation that I knew nothing.

The professor took the stand that day and said these words, "Was the Garden of Eden God's original plan, or was it a Divine Sting Operation?" My jaw hit the floor, I began to sweat, my heart began to pound, and I wondered if I should debate with my professor on day one. I couldn't take it anymore! I had to say something! "What do you mean by a Divine Sting Operation?" I asked. "Are you actually suggesting that God set us up to sin?" I continued. What I did not know at the time was that this professor's particular style of teaching was to say things to make us mad enough to wrestle with Scripture for ourselves... and for me it worked.

I was absolutely furious. There were times when people wouldn't want to hang around me because all I would talk about was what this professor had said or done in class. There came a point when the heat became so intense in class that I just didn't know if I could take it anymore. The lessons weren't clicking for me, and I thought to myself, "If I can't understand this, how can I be a preacher of it? How can I teach and preach something that I just don't get?" What I didn't realize was that I was glass in the fire. I was being prepared, purified, and softened so that God could create within me the character needed to be successful in ministry for the long haul.

One night all of my friends were getting ready to go out to a movie. I declined their invitation to join them so I could stay in my room to take care of some unfinished business with God. This was a turning point, not only in my college career, but in my life. I was truly in a battle with my own beliefs. I didn't know if I wanted to believe this anymore or not. My passion for God had dwindled to a small spark all because no one warned me about the crucible of the classroom. That night I walked into my room, shut the door, and picked a fight with God.

I opened the window of my second-story room which faced the northern sky, raised my fist up defiantly toward heaven, and vented all of my frustrations. Why couldn't I understand it all? Why couldn't I get the answers to every single question I had? Why was there ambiguity in certain areas of Scripture? I told God that night, in my anger, that if he could not reveal the answers to me then I was done, not only with my call to ministry, but done with Him.

At that point I sensed the presence of the Holy Spirit in the room, and I hit my knees in total fear and humility. The words that had poured from my lips that night were not the words of wisdom but of folly. I began to weep as I asked God to forgive me. Just then, I noticed my Bible lying on my bed. I went over to my bedside, knelt down, picked up my Bible, and said to God, "I may not understand everything, but I choose now to trust you and believe that in your time you will reveal your truth to me." Freedom flooded that room and my heart. I knew that I had made the best choice of my life, and I have never looked back since.

-CONCLUSION-

- Bringing It Home -

You will come to that point if you remain in Christian college for any length of time. You will be challenged far beyond your imagination. And when that happens, what are you going to do? Christian College will have many crucibles to experience, and each one is necessary to your growth and maturity. But the choice to persevere through them is yours to make. Following the seven strategies in this book helped me to walk through the fire of Christian college and come out on the other end refined, and I am positive they will do the same for you.

These strategies are…

1. Exercising Extreme Faith
2. Developing A Vibrant Prayer Life
3. Picking Wise Friendships
4. Having Appropriate Levels of Ministry Involvement
5. Not Shortcutting The Process of Bible School
6. Never Selling Out Your Name or Your Word
7. Always Walking In Humility

You will be tried by fire in Christian college, but by applying the strategies set forth in this book, in the end you will be a masterpiece in the hands of our Creator.

As the author, I am eternally blessed that you have allowed me to walk with you during this brief season in your life. I am praying for your total success in Christian college, life, and ministry.

-TRIED BY FIRE-

Whether you are called to be a doctor, lawyer, veterinarian, pastor, missionary, or teacher, I am praying that you do it all with the passion and fire of God in your heart.

- 2 Timothy 1:6 -
"For this reason I remind you to fan into flame the gift of God, which is in you..."

CHAPTER 1
NOTES

-1 Samuel 13 (NIV)

-1 Samuel 14:6 (NIV)

CHAPTER 2
NOTES

-Daniel 1:8 (NIV)

-Daniel 6:2 (ESV)

-Daniel 6:3 (ESV)

-Daniel 6:4 (NIV)

-Daniel 6:5 (ESV)

-Daniel 6:10 (NIV)

-Daniel 6:24 (NIV)

-Collins, Jim. Good To Great. New York: HarperCollins
       Publishers Inc., 2001.

CHAPTER 3
NOTES

-1 Corinthians 15:33 (NIV)

-1 Samuel 27:1-3 (NIV)

-1 Samuel 30:6 (NIV)

-Mark 1:35 (NIV)

-Proverbs 16:7 (NIV)

CHAPTER 4
NOTES

-1 Kings 19:16 (NKJV)

-1 Kings 19:19 (NKJV)

-2 Kings 3:11 (NKJV)

-Ecclesiastes 3:1 (NIV)

-Philippians 4:6 (NIV)

-James 3:1 9 (NIV)

-2 Timothy 1:6 (NIV)

CHAPTER 5
NOTES

-Genesis 39:6-8; 12 (NIV)

-Genesis 50:20 (NIV)

-Genesis 39:23 (NIV)

-I Corinthians 10:13

-Jeremiah 20:9 (NIV)

-Ecclesiastes 3:1 (NIV)

CHAPTER 6
NOTES

-1 Kings 21:2-3 (NIV)

-Proverbs 10:22 (KJV)

CHAPTER 7

NOTES

-Proverbs 16:18 (NIV)

-1 Corinthians 3:7 (NIV)

-Acts 14:11-15 (NIV)

-Cartledge, Don. Personal INTERVIEW. 4 May 2009.

CONCLUSION

NOTES

-Proverbs 17:3 (KJV)

-2 Timothy 1:6 (NIV)

ABOUT
THE AUTHOR

Daniel Day is first and foremost a passionate follower of Jesus Christ. He is also a husband, father, and minister of the Gospel. He has degrees from Central Bible College which include a B.A. in Preaching and Evangelism as well as an A.A. in both Pastoral Ministries and Biblical Studies.

While attending Christian college, he received the Outstanding Preaching and Evangelism Major and Outstanding Senior of the Year awards. Daniel was also chosen to deliver the commencement address at his graduation ceremony in May of 2007.

He has served as the full-time Youth Pastor of Harvest Christian Center since 2007. Daniel lives with his wife, Sara, and daughter, Mikayla, in El Paso, Texas.

ABOUT
THE BOOK

90% of the proceeds from this book will go to support missionaries around the world, church planting, and providing scholarships for college students.

For more information or to make a donation visit www.thestokedbook.com.

ORDER INFORMATION:
To place an order visit www.thestokedbook.com. Bulk discounts are available.

THE STOKED SEMINAR

The Stoked Seminar is a high impact series that highlights the 7 Strategies discussed throughout the book.

The 7 Strategies Include:

Extraordinary Faith

A Powerful Prayer Life

Godly Friendships

Personal Investment

Resisting Temptation

Never Selling Out

Reflecting All Glory To Jesus Christ

If your school or church would like to book a STOKED Seminar for your college group or graduating high school seniors, you can email info@thestokedbook.com.

Design & Layout provided by

For more info visit NickPooleNow.com